Terrific Twos

Positive view on toddler's discipline. Effective tips and working strategies for parents.

Your Free Gift

I wanted to show my appreciation that you support my work so I've put together a free gift for you.

Bonus – Daily Routine for Toddlers

Just visit the link above to download it now.

I know you will love this gift.

Thanks!

Merry Palmer

Introduction

With a nickname like the Terrible Twos, the toddler stage is one parents look forward to and dread. You want to survive this stage with your toddler successfully, but you also want them to thrive and learn at the same time. Many parents feel like they're going to lose their mind at this stage of their baby's development, but rest assured, you're not the only one.

There's no such thing as a perfect parent, even if you strive as hard as you can toward being one, so don't beat yourself up if you make mistakes or have a few awful thoughts run through your head. It's time for parents to stand up and be honest about what happens when a baby hits the age of two, give or take a few months. It's also time new parents were told the truth about what's happening with their baby and how to handle it, rather than just giving the stage a terrible nickname.

Before you learn about how to socialize and discipline your child at this stage, let's look at what's happening inside of them physically, emotionally, and mentally. Understanding where they're coming from can help you tailor your discipline style to what is most healthy for your baby.

Physically, your baby is constantly improving their fine and gross motor skills. Around this age, your child will be able to jump up with both their feet leaving the ground, which leaves a lot of room for getting in trouble. Your baby can now climb the stairs and hold onto the railing, which is one of the most frightening things a parent can go through.

On a much cuter note, your baby can now make scribbles and straight lines with a pencil, and your child will begin to show whether they're going to be a righty or a lefty. Your baby can feed him or herself well, but that doesn't mean your baby will be neat or willing to do this at first. Your baby can also stack blocks pretty high. All of these things are amazing to watch for parents, but they're also frightening because it means more opportunities to get in trouble or get hurt.

Let's be honest here. Your toddler is going to get a few bumps and bruises. Just as they were falling down as they were beginning to learn how to walk, and just as they were bumping their heads or their appendages on furniture, they will still do the same thing. It might be tempting to wrap your child in foam and duct tape to keep him or her safe, but it's not necessary.

Behaviorally, this is the stage most parents dread because of the nickname this part of your baby's life was given. There are some days you might feel like you're going through the Terrible Twos firsthand, especially when your child's throwing a tantrum. However, remember you're not alone because all children go through this stage. They're normal for this age group, and it's part of the process of your child trying to become more independent.

Tantrums are also a sign your child is not fully aware of what their emotions are yet, or they haven't fully developed the verbal skills to express how they're feeling. A good way to handle this is to distract your child, but we'll get into that a little later. Just keep in mind your toddler's behavior is not all bad. Your baby still loves physical affection, will return your hugs and kisses, and will blossom if you continue to be patient and loving toward them.

No, it won't all be sunshine and rainbows with a toddler, but you can help your toddler grow and lessen your stress levels if you know how to handle the difficult situations that arise. In this book, you'll learn about why your toddler is suddenly pushing your boundaries, why discipline is important, and what discipline is appropriate for your toddler.

Most importantly, you will learn you are not alone in this, and there are healthy ways for both you and your child to cope during this stage. Instead of thinking of the toddler stage as the Terrible Twos, let's rethink it as the Terrific Twos!

Chapter One – What's with 'No!'?

Every parent goes through it, and the first time they hear the word from their adorable toddler, they automatically think, "Oh no, it's the Terrible Twos. We've reached that milestone."

It's all right; every parent goes through this stage with their child because it's an absolutely normal phase of development. However, that doesn't mean you have to suffer for very long. There are many ways you can help your child get through this very emotionally charged period of their life.

The technical term for this fascination with the word 'no' is known as refusal to child psychologists, and the simple fact is your toddler is saying this word just because they can. Your toddler's discovered they have a will, and they want to exercise it to the best of their ability, which means saying 'no' to the one person who has told them what to do their entire life – you.

It probably seems this phase has come on overnight, and it really does happen suddenly, leaving you confused as to why your child has suddenly become defiant. Thankfully, the stage can disappear as quickly as it came on, and you're left with the 'I don't know' or 'Maybe' stage. However, while you're waiting for your toddler to make it through this stage, you can experiment with a few coping strategies to make it a little easier.

Offer Your Toddler Choices

In reality, this is all your toddler is asking for. They're in the mood to make their own decisions rather than have Mom and Dad play tyrant, so play nice and give them a few choices! For example,

- Do you want juice or milk today?

- Do you want to wear the purple or pink shoes?

- Do you want to play nice with your friend, or do you want to play alone?

- Do you want to wear the pants or the skirt?

Just make sure you don't offer your toddler more than two options, and never offer them an option you don't want to follow through with. If you don't want them to wear the red shoes, then don't offer them. If your toddler is indecisive, counting is a good motivator, too: "I'm going to count to five and then you choose something, or I'm going to choose for you."

You have to be careful with how often you use this option because your toddler will become immune to it eventually.

Offer an Appearance of Options

There are moments where you can't offer your toddler another option, so you have to offer the appearance of one. To do this properly, you need to keep two important things in mind: you know more than your child does, and just about anything can be turned into a choice. Let's look at some examples.

- "Would you like to stay in the car for two minutes and play or get out of the car now?" Either way, your child is going to end up getting out of the car.

- "Would you prefer we put the sweater on backward or frontward?" Since both of you understand your child most likely won't want to wear the sweater backward, you're adding some humor to the situation. However, if your child says they want to wear it backward, then you need to let them wear it backward. Never go back on a choice when they've made it.

Start Teaching Other Responses

One of the reasons your toddler is saying this word so much is because they don't know a lot of other words, and you've most likely said this one to them a lot. Help your toddler expand their vocabulary by turning the word 'no' into a game.

When your toddler says 'no,' ask him or her what the opposite of 'no' is. When he or she says 'no,' ask them what comes in between 'no' and 'yes,' and if they don't know, tell them – maybe, perhaps, and possibly. If your toddler has a tendency to say 'no' rudely, then have them say 'no, thank you' instead. And for the chatty toddlers out there who say 'no' rudely, have them say 'no, thank you very much.'

You could make their 'no' response a little less automatic and possibly get a yes if you set up the situation with something silly, such as asking your child, "What would a dog say if you said, 'Mr. Dog, would you want a bone?'" When your toddler says, "Yes," you'd follow up with, "And what would you say if I asked you if you wanted to eat your peas?" Hopefully, your toddler will be giggling enough that he or she will be too happy to rebuff the peas.

Limit Your Use of the Word 'No.'

Your toddler might be screaming 'no' at the top of their lungs all the time because he or she is constantly hearing that word from you, and it's most likely directed at them. If this is the cause of the issue, then you should try to use alternative words to 'no' instead.

Some examples of this might be:

- Uh-uh
- Nope
- Nay
- Nah
- No way
- Negative
- Out of the question
- Under no circumstances
- Not likely
- Thumbs down
- Go fish

One way to do this is to use words that are more specific to the situation that's happening. For example, "We don't hit other people," or, "It's time to use your indoor voice, please."

Be Firm

There are going to be times that no matter what you do to avoid or distract your toddler from the situation, you'll end up in a showdown. If your toddler stops in the middle of the street and refuses to move any further, you'll move your toddler quickly. But safety concerns aren't the only reason to be firm with a toddler. A toddler has a will, but you can't allow your toddler to exert that will all the time. It'll get messy very quickly.

It's perfectly fine for you, as a parent, to say, "This isn't a time when I can give you an option. There're no options now. I know you don't want to do this, or you don't like this, and I'm sorry about that, but this is the way it has to be." And when your toddler asks why, you respond with, "Because I'm your mommy/daddy."

Despite all these strategies, you'll still have to wait out this stage. Thankfully, it won't last forever, and with some of these strategies in place, it'll be a little less of a time period before you get back into the swing of agreeing with each other.

Chapter Two – How to Talk to Your Toddler

Everyone talks about their one-year-old in front of them to other parents, their spouse, friends, and anyone else who will listen. Who doesn't recount a day's events to their spouse while they're having dinner, or compare their kids' personalities with other parents at playgroup? Since young children are around their parents all the time, it's nearly impossible to save all child-related chatter for when the child is sleeping or playing. Adults often assume that because a child doesn't talk much or say words very well, they're not taking in what adults are saying. That's wrong. Your baby is listening, and they understand a lot more than you think.

Often, there's a huge difference between expressive language and receptive language at the toddler stage. Toddlers can understand a complex conversation much earlier than most parents believe. For example, your baby will recognize his or her name by the time they're four and a half months old, so young babies might pay more attention if you mention their name in conversation. By fourteen months, your baby will be a master at reading your social cues. When you're angry, your voice is louder. When you're happy, you tend to speak softly and breathe slower.

No matter what you're saying, your toddler understands the underlying message. If you complain about your child taking off their diaper but think it's cute, your baby hears a voice with a nice tone. If you're angry about it, your child will hear the anger in your tone.

By the time your baby turns one, most of them know around fifty words. They are simple nouns that will refer to people or objects, such as mommy, daddy, dog, and so on and so forth. Within the next several months, they will begin to put the nouns with verbs and begin to understand sentences.

Then, when they are between eighteen to twenty-one months, they will suddenly launch into a stage known as the language explosion. They will learn an average of nine words a day, and they will start to understand how the word order affects the meaning. Once this occurs, your toddler will begin to figure out not just when you're talking about them, but also what you're saying about them. For example, if your toddler hears you complain about how he pulled on the dog's ears, he'll most likely pick up on his name and the word dog, but he'll also understand you believe he did something bad.

So do you need to curtail what you're saying when your toddler is in the room? Yes and no. Toddlers who have parents who talk about them in a tender, loving way enjoy the attention. Your toddler should be included in your conversations when they are in the room. It makes much more sense to be talking with them rather than around them because this helps strengthen their language skills and their interaction skills at the same time.

However, it's important that you keep negative things you say around your toddler to a minimum. If toddlers hear you always say something about them in a negative fashion, such as, "Katie's a bully," then they can carry that around for a long time. Studies have shown that children can learn words or phrases without knowing what they mean, and then piecing that meaning together at a later date. So if a child is always being called a bully, then that child might take that label on as part of their identity once the meaning has been deciphered.

Still, even sensitive parents will make this mistake and talk about their toddler in front of them from time to time. As long as it isn't all the time, you're not doing terrible damage, but you should be careful. If you wouldn't want that thing said about you, then don't say it in front of your child. Toddlers are little people, no matter how small they are, and they are very impressionable.

So how should you be talking to your toddler?

Tips for Addressing Your Toddler Correctly

1.   **Connect before directing.** Before you direct your toddler on how to do something or what they should be doing, you should be getting down to their eye level and engaging them with some eye contact to get their attention. Teach your toddler how to focus by saying their name and telling them what you want them to do in order to focus on you, such as, "Katie, I need you to look at me," or "Billy, I need you to listen to me." Offer the same body language when you're listening to your child. Be sure you don't make your eye contact so intense your child perceives you to be controlling rather than connecting with them.

2.   **Address your child.** Open your request with their name, such as "Helen, please…"

3.   **Be brief.** You should have a one-sentence rule. The longer you keep talking, the more likely your toddler will forget what it was they were supposed to do. They'll begin to tune you out. So put your directive in the first sentence you say to your child. Too much talking gives your child the impression you're not sure what you want to say, and if she can keep you talking, then she or he can sidetrack you.

4.   **Keep it simple.** Use one-syllable words and keep your sentences short. Listen to how your toddler communicates with other toddlers and take note of that. When your child looks disinterested or has a glazed look, then you're not being understood.

5.   **Ask your toddler to repeat the request.** If your child can't repeat it back to you, then your request is too complicated or too long.

6.   **Make an offer they can't refuse.** You can reason with toddlers, especially if you want to avoid power struggles. Something such as, "Get dressed so you can play," offers a reason for your child to perform the action.

7.   **Be positive.** Instead of telling your child to, "Stop yelling," say, "We use our inside voice inside."

8.   **Begin directives with "I want."** Rather than tell your child to get down, tell them, "I want you to get down." Rather than, "Give Terry a turn," say, "I want you to give Terry a turn now." This works with toddlers who want to please you but don't want to be ordered around. By saying, "I want," you're giving a reason for complying rather than just ordering your toddler to do something.

9.   **"When…Then."** Say, "When you brush your teeth, then we'll read the story," Or, "When you finish picking up your toys, then we can go outside to play." The word 'when' implies you expect your toddler to listen and obey and works better than the word 'if' because it suggests to your child that they have a choice when you don't intend to.

10.   **Actions First, Words Second.** Instead of telling your child it's soon time for dinner from the other room, walk into the room where your child is playing and get down to their level. Quietly and firmly tell your child it's almost time for dinner, and then get involved with your child's interest for a few minutes. Going to your toddler tells them you're serious about the request; otherwise, it looks like a preference.

11.   **Give them choices.** "Do you want to put on your PJs first, or brush your teeth first?" "Do you want the red shirt or the blue shirt?"

12.   **Speak to your child according to their development level.** The younger your toddler is, the shorter and simpler your requests should be. Consider your toddler's level of understanding. As an example, many parents will ask their three-year-old why they did something. Most adults can't even answer that question, so why expect your three-

year-old to answer it? Instead, say something along the lines of, "Let's talk about what just happened."

13. **Speak socially correct to your toddler.** Even two-year-olds understand the concept of 'please.' Expect politeness from your toddler. Children shouldn't feel that manners are optional. Speak to your child the way you'd want them to speak to you.

14. **Speak psychologically right.** Judgment openers and threats are likely to make your child defensive. 'You' messages will make your child clam-up. 'I' message are not accusing. Rather than saying, "You'd better put your toys away…" or, "You must put your toys away…," try, "I would like it if you…" or, "I'm so happy (or pleased) when you…" Instead of saying, "You need to brush your teeth," say, "I need you to brush your teeth." Don't ask leading questions when negative answers aren't an option. "Will you pick up your toys please?" Just say, "Pick up your toys, please."

15. **Write it down.** Reminders easily evolve into nagging, especially for a preteen who might not respond to being told to do something over and over again. Without saying a word, you can communicate everything you have to say. Talk with a paper and pen. Leave a humorous note for a child old enough to read, and sit back and watch what you want being done.

16. **Talk your child down.** The louder your child is yelling, then the softer you should be responding. Let your child vent while you interject some soft comments, such as, "I understand," and, "Let me help." Sometimes, just being a caring listener winds down the tantrum your toddler is having. If you come in at their level, you have two tantrums to handle: yours and his or hers.

17. **Settle listeners.** Before you tell your toddler to do something, restore emotional balance. Otherwise, you're

wasting time. Nothing will sink in when your toddler is an emotional wreck.

18.   **Replay the message.** Toddlers have to be told to do something a lot. Children who are under two have a hard time remembering your orders. Most three-year-olds will start to internalize your orders so they sink in. Do less and less repeating as your child becomes older. Preteens will regard your repetition as nagging.

19.   **Let your toddler complete your thought.** Rather than saying, "Don't leave your toys out," try, "Lauren, think of where you'd like to put your toys." Letting your child fill in the blanks can create a lasting lesson.

20.   **Use rhyming rules.** "If you hit, you sit." Have your child repeat them. It's easier for rhyming rules to sink in.

21.   **Give a likable alternative when you can.** "You can't go to the park alone, but you can play in the back yard."

22.   **Give your toddler advanced notice.** "We're going to be leaving soon. Say goodbye to your toys, goodbye to your sister, goodbye to grandpa…"

23.   **Open up a closed off toddler.** Carefully chosen phrases will open up your toddler's closed off mind and mouth. Stick to topics you know your child will become excited about. Ask a question that requires more than just a yes or a no. Stick to the specifics. Rather than, "Did you have a good day at school," try, "What's the most interesting thing you did today at school?"

24.   **"When you…I feel…Because…"** "When you run out into the road, Daddy feels scared because you could get hit."

25.   **End the discussion.** If matters are really closed to discussing them, then say so. "I'm not going to change my mind about this. I'm sorry." You'll save a lot of time, as well

as wear and tear on both you and your child. However, reserve this for only when you really mean it.

Specific Examples

Let's look at a few specific examples to give you some more ideas about how to handle a situation with your toddler.

You're feeling really frustrated right now.

When you realize your toddler's about to have a tantrum, you can often get them to calm down and listen by kneeling down, looking into their eyes, and labeling their emotions for them. When you say, "That made you upset," you'll help him or her understand it's normal to experience strong and sometimes frightening emotions. Your words help them process the emotions they're feeling, and when they're a little older, they'll be able to say, "I'm upset," or, "I'm really happy," all by themselves.

Stop, that's hot.

If you want to make a point about something being dangerous, then keep it short and simple. Use only three to four words. Parents will over-explain a situation and the meaning gets lost in all those words. It's okay to use a firm, "No," when you need to get their attention immediately if they're going to hurt themselves or someone else. But if your child constantly hears the word 'no,' then he or she will start to tune it out. If that's already happened, you need to baby-proof your house so your child can explore without always hearing reprimands.

It's time to take a bath now.

Many parents will make the mistake of asking their child if they want to do something, but it's better to use statements when you need your child to transition into another activity, such as taking a bath. When you inquire about something, you are giving your child a choice, which opens up the normal routine to being a conflict. The rule you need to follow is not to ask, just tell when there isn't really an option.

First...Then...

Your toddler has some foggy notions about time, so when you tell your toddler you're going to do something in fifteen minutes, it doesn't mean much to them. Rather than giving them a time frame, describe the sequence of events. For example, "First we're going to clean up, and then we're going to get dressed, so we're ready to go."

Do your socks go on first, or do your pants go on first?

Let your child make the simpler choices as part of their daily routine. When you hand over just a tad bit of control, you're boosting their confidence when they get to do something. However, a choice between just two items is enough. Younger kids have limited memory and attention spans, and they just can't keep track of everything.

You're throwing food; all done.

To manage a toddler's behavior at the table, you need to act quickly and use the same short phrases every time. If your toddler has a tendency to throw food, then use a simple phrase like the one listed above. Keep a calm tone, and then remove your toddler from the table to get them away from the situation.

I like how you held my hand when we were in the busy store.

Positive reinforcement, pointing out what they did right, is a strong motivator for them. Even if they don't completely understand, your toddler will pick up on the rhythm and the cadence with which you say the words, and they will understand some of the meaning.

Let's name the animals in the book.

You're most likely teaching your toddler to name simple things, such as body parts, colors, and foods, but finding more subjects to talk about with them helps them make new language connections. Remember, they can learn a lot of words in just one day. Point out different objects in the books you read to them every time you read the book together. While you're in the park, use descriptive words. Instead of saying, "Look at that tree," say, "Look at that tall tree with red leaves." This helps them see the world in a new way.

Some of the important takeaways you should remember from this chapter are:

- Do not use baby talk with your toddler. They are learning a lot of information on a daily basis, and speaking to them in an adult manner teaches them how to socialize and interact on a higher level.

- Never give your toddler a choice when there isn't really a choice, and keep choices down to just two. Your toddler only has so many reasoning skills right now, and giving them a choice when there isn't one is just unfair.

- Your toddler is amazing and can understand the words you're saying around them, even if they're not forming those words into sentences themselves yet. Watch what you're saying around them.

Chapter Three – The Importance of Discipline

Disciplining your child is just as important as everything else you're teaching them, and sometimes, it's just necessary. This is the part of parenting most parents dread. They see discipline as a negative action because, when they were growing up, discipline was negative for them. However, you can choose how you discipline your toddler, and it doesn't have to be in line with what your parents may have done, or it can be! That's the beauty of having a child; you get to choose how you raise them.

Before we take a look at the proper methods of discipline for a toddler and the improper ones, let's look at some of the benefits of discipline. Let's shine a new light on this word that's perceived to be negative by many people.

Helps Children Manage Anxiety

As much as they might look like they want to be, your toddler doesn't really want to be in control. They test the limits to make sure their parents are going to keep them safe! When an adult offers positive and negative consequences for an action, it will help the child learn and grow.

Toddlers who have permissive parents will feel anxiety because they're managing their decisions all the time. They never have any direction. Children know they're not able to make the best choices all the time and they want to learn from you what decisions they should make. The lack of guidance and help tends to create feelings of anxiety rather than comfort.

Teaches Good Decision-Making

The right discipline will teach your toddler how to make better decisions. As an example, when a child loses the privilege to ride their bike because they rode into the road, they will learn to make safer decisions the next time they're riding their bike.

Healthy discipline will provide your toddler with the chance to think about their actions and recognize an alternative solution to the problem. Toddlers need to learn problem-solving skills, so they can understand the possible consequences of their behavior and actions.

It's imperative to distinguish the difference between punishments and consequences. When children are disciplined with the right consequences, they will learn from their mistakes. Punishments will tend to teach your toddler you're mean, or they learn how to 'not get caught' when they do something wrong.

Discipline Teaches Them to Manage Emotions

Discipline will help your child learn how to manage their feelings in a positive manner. For example, when your toddler receives a timeout for hitting their playmate, they learn a valuable skill to help them manage their frustration in the future. The goal is for your child to learn to take a time out on their own when they feel really upset.

Other strategies, such as praise, teach your children how to handle their emotions. For example, "You're working really hard to build that tower despite it being really hard to do. Keep up your good work." This helps motivate them to tolerate frustrations and keep going without giving up and accepting failure.

Ignoring is a good way to teach your child how to manage their frustrations, too. When you ignore a temper tantrum, your child will learn this isn't a good way to get what they desire. Ignoring other behaviors, like whining, will show that these attention-seeking actions aren't working and they'll need to find another way to meet their needs when they feel upset.

Discipline Keeps Them Safe

The main goal of disciplining your child should always be to keep them safe. This includes major issues, such as looking both directions before they cross the street, or not riding their bicycle in the street. There should be consequences for your child when they're not taking the right safety precautions.

Discipline ought to address other health issues, such as preventing becoming obese. If you allow your child to eat whatever they want whenever they want, this will create some serious health conditions because children are not able to make healthy choices for themselves without your guidance.

When you use an authoritative approach and tell your child the underlying reason for why they shouldn't do something, it helps them learn to examine the safety issues of an action before they do it. For example, rather than saying, "Get down from there," when your child is jumping on their bed, it might be helpful to let them know it's a safety risk and they could get hurt. This teaches them to look for a potential safety issue in other situations.

Core Components of Healthy Discipline

When most parents think about discipline, they think about punishment. But effective discipline is more than just losing a privilege or having a time-out. In fact, these consequences are not likely to be effective if they're the bulk of your discipline focuses because they're negative. Healthy discipline needs to contain five core components.

#1 Healthy Relationship with Your Toddler

If you don't have a healthy relationship with your toddler, then discipline isn't going to work.

Toddlers are more motivated to listen to what their parents are saying when they respect their parent's decision. The need for having a healthy relationship with your child stems beyond just you. Teachers, step-parents, and daycare providers are much more effective when they have healthy relationships with your child, too.

#2 Discipline's a Teaching Tool

If discipline is just reserved for correcting bad behavior, it's not going to be very effective. If you find you're always saying, "Don't do that," and, "It's time-out time," without teaching them the right behavior, then they won't learn. That means your toddler is more likely to repeat that mistake in the future.

To really help your toddler change their behavior, discipline should be a teaching tool. That means helping your toddler identify what to do. Rather than telling your toddler not to hit their brother, make sure you invest time in teaching your toddler to resolve the conflict peacefully.

#3 Be Consistent

If you only put your toddler into time-out one out of every ten times they hit their sibling, then your toddler's not going to stop hitting their sibling. After all, it's worth the risk of performing the behavior if there's only a ten percent chance they're going to get into trouble.

If you want discipline to be effective, then you have to be consistent.

If you put your child in time-out for hitting every time they hit, then your child will link their behavior with the consequence. Over time, your child will realize that this behavior leads to a consequence they don't like.

#4 Be Immediate
Being prompt about a consequence will help your toddler connect the dots between behavior and consequences. If a toddler doesn't lose their park privileges for a day for hitting someone at the park, then the consequence is not as effective.

There might be times when you can't have an immediate consequence for something. Sometimes, you might not realize your toddler has broken the rules until hours or days later. In these instances, a late consequence is the only option. However, it's important to avoid saying things such as, "Wait until your mother/father gets home," because a consequence that's given hours later is going to be less effective.

#5 Be Fair
If your toddler forgets to put their toys away before bed, and you keep them from playing with those toys for an entire week, your toddler won't perceive this to be a fair consequence. Therefore, your toddler might try to sneak in play when you're not around. Your toddler won't abide by the consequence if they don't think it's fair.

When kids are convinced they're being served injustice, then they will fight you every step of the way. That doesn't mean you need to negotiate with your toddler and give in when they protest about the consequence, but it does mean you should make sure your punishments are not overly harsh.

So remember, discipline is important because it teaches your child to be safe, how to manage their emotions, and keeps them feeling secure. Now, let's look at some of the common discipline mistakes parent make with their toddlers.

Chapter Four – Common Discipline Mistakes Parents Make

Before you learn how to discipline your child appropriately, let's talk about some of the common mistakes parents tend to make. In this section, you'll learn some of the common thoughts or emotions parents go through when they discipline, and how these thoughts and emotions can interfere with discipline correctly.

"He/she's been under a lot of stress, and I feel sorry for him/her."

Parents often feel guilty when their toddler has to go through a tough time, such as being bullied in school or going through a divorce. It's natural for a parent to feel bad, because who wants to see their child hurt?

Allowing bad behavior to slide, though, is not the solution. In fact, a stressed out child needs discipline more than ever for them to feel secure. Show your child you can still keep them safe by sticking to the limits.

"He/she didn't mean to do that."

Children should not be disciplined for spilling a glass of milk by accident, but they should still take responsibility for their actions through helping to clean up the milk. Letting too much leeway happen because something was an accident prevents your toddler from accepting responsibility for the accident.

If you decide your toddler didn't mean to push the other child too hard and excuse this action, then your toddler will learn they can talk their way out things by using the, 'it was an accident,' excuse.

"I didn't spend enough time with him/her lately."

Letting your child misbehave because of your guilt doesn't do anyone any good. If you feel guilty, look for another way to resolve that guilt rather than absolving it by not using discipline. For example, do you need to set more time aside to spend with your toddler? Do you need to remind yourself it's good for your child to have healthy discipline?

"I was too hard on him/her yesterday."

If you offered a discipline that was too harsh earlier, it doesn't mean they get to do whatever they want now. It's essential you're consistent with discipline. Inconsistency will only confuse your toddler and lead to more behavioral issues in the future.

"Kids are just kids."

There's a thing such as normal misbehavior from toddlers, but it's important to distinguish this normal misbehavior from abnormal misbehavior. Letting your toddler get away with misbehavior by excusing it as normal kid stuff is detrimental if you're allowing your toddler to get away with too many violations of the rules.

"I don't want him/her to be upset."

Sometimes, it's tempting to allow your toddler to get away with something when they're having a good time and you know putting him or her in time-out is going to upset them. However, teaching them to deal with their negative emotions is one of the six life skills they have to be taught. You'll do your toddler a disservice by not helping them learn how to regulate their emotions.

"I'm too tired to handle this."
There are going to be days where you just feel too tired or weary to dish out one more undesirable consequence. However, it's imperative you get the energy to offer your toddler consistent discipline. Devote some extra time and energy to behavior issues now and avoid more issues down the road.

"He/she won't listen anyway."
Lacking confidence in parenting is a huge problem that prevents you from disciplining because you're afraid your child won't go to time out or they won't listen to you when a privilege is taken away. If a consequence is not effective, then examine the reason why your discipline isn't working. Avoiding it only makes the problem worse, and it's essential you gain parenting skills to discipline properly.

"He'll/she'll think I'm mean."
One of the largest parenting mistakes parents make is only to look at the short-term. In the short-term, your toddler could think you're mean for taking away their toy or putting them in time out. However, in the long-run, it's better for them and essential for them to learn. Sometimes, when your toddler is upset with you, it means you're doing your job as a parent.

"I always need to be the bad guy."
If your partner always allows your toddler to get away with behavioral issues, then it's likely you'll feel you're the bad guy when you discipline your toddler. Learn how to discipline together as a team, so your toddler doesn't view one person as the 'bad guy.' Establish some household rules and work together to enforce them.

You threaten to use time-out, and then don't follow through.
Here's why this doesn't work. Your toddler will realize you don't mean what you say, and they'll lose all respect for what you say to

them. Idle threats will cause more problems than solving them. Your goal shouldn't be for your toddler to fear you, but it should be for them to respect you. Typically, a time-out threat is made with a louder tone because parents believe that if they yell, their children will hear them. That's not true. They often just learn to tune you out.

If you threaten to use time-out with your toddler, do so with a firm, but emotionless, voice. Be prepared to follow through with the threat, no matter where you're located. There are plenty of places for you to find a time-out space for your toddler. It could be on the bench at the mall, or in the entranceway of the restaurant (off to one side, of course). Having to stop what you're doing might be inconvenient for you, but in the long-term, always following through makes time-outs more effective.

You lecture or yell while your child is in time-out.

Children need time to process while they're in time-out. No one can do that when they're being yelled at. You want them to understand what they did wrong and realize why they shouldn't do that in the future. Yelling makes them feel upset and angry about being in time-out, and it distracts them from the point of a time-out, which is to think about what they did.

Stay calm when you put them in a time-out. You shouldn't ever yell at your child because you model behavior to them that you wouldn't want them to model back. Stay calm and model this emotional balance for them. As a parent, there will be times when you want to scream, but it causes long-term damage that could undo the trust you've built with your child, so it's not worth it.

Your child is in time-out for too long or too short of a period of time.

Time-outs don't work for toddlers who are fidgety and under the age of two, and most experts will agree that attempting this type of discipline on anyone younger is just pointless. Time-outs are originally a way for your child to take a break, think about what they did wrong, and maybe feel a little remorse about it. Then they settle down and return to their normal activities. They don't make sense for children below the age of two.

Certain experts recommend time-outs be a length directly correlated to your child's age, so two minutes for a two-year-old, three for a three-year-old, and so on and so forth. However, some believe in equity for kids of any age. After the age of two, time-outs should be five minutes for everyone. Time-out shouldn't start until your child is quiet, too. Every child is going to be different, so an incredibly active-three-year-old might have trouble sitting in a time-out for five minutes, so feel free to modify the rules based on your child's situation. The important thing is to find something that works for them and be consistent.

You're emotional when you put your child in time-out.
If your child understands they're causing you pain when you put them in time-out, then they will prolong the pain and keep disrupting time-out so that it's punishment for you, too. They want power over you because they don't want you to have any power over them. Therefore, don't put your child in time-out when you're emotional or hysterical. Be quick, firm, and allow them to know you mean business. If they continually disrupt time-out, then don't berate them or act as if they're inconveniencing you. Just help them understand they're adding time to their time-out session.

Your toddler really wants a time-out.
You might be wondering why in the world your toddler would want a time-out, but some good examples might be while they're at the grocery store in a boring situation, or when they're doing something they don't like in the first place. Your toddler might jump at the opportunity to sit in a time-out rather than walk through the aisles of the grocery store one more time.

So how do you handle that situation? You don't do the time-out right then and there. Just make sure the time-out happens as soon as you get home, and let them know the reason as to why they're in a time-out briefly before it starts. Just make sure you follow through with the time-out!

You put your toddler in their room during a time-out.

Children's rooms are usually a fun place for them to go. They have all their toys, games, and entertainment areas there, which prevents them from reflecting on their bad behavior, which is the whole point of time-out. Therefore, time-out should be in a 'boring' area of the home. A chair facing the blank wall will work, but some people find this a little too harsh.

If you don't like the blank wall idea, then try having a designated room for a time-out. The laundry room is a good place. And if they're really bored, maybe they'll fold that extra load for you! Of course, you should always watch your child wherever they are and make sure the room is safe for them.

You don't give your toddler a lot of time-in.

The point of time-out is to withdraw positive reinforcement. If your toddler isn't accustomed to regular praise from you and doesn't have a strong bond with you, then nothing is being taken away from them during this time. Encourage positive behavior with your toddler. When your toddler does something you enjoy, let him or her know! This gives them a positive feeling when they behave appropriately, and wrong when they don't. This motivates your toddler to behave more positively.

You discipline your toddler with attitude.

Do you know a parent who tends to yell, become snippy, exaggerate, and just become mean to their kids when they want them to behave? Are you one of those parents? This behavior is not conducive to getting your toddler to behave positively. Rather than using consequences to discipline a toddler, you or someone you know is using attitude.

It's almost as if parents who discipline this way are trying to achieve emotional catharsis through raising their voice, displaying contempt, and losing their temper. However, research has shown that venting emotionally doesn't make you feel better, so it's no use to you or your child.

The first reason you shouldn't use attitude to discipline a child is that it teaches them that someone who doesn't get what they want should respond by losing their cool. Sure, when your toddler is misbehaving and throwing a fit, you might feel you have a perfectly good reason to lose your temper. They're being bad. However, to them, you're losing it because you're not getting them to act the way you would prefer. Therefore, when they don't get what they want, they'll behave the same way.

The second reason is it doesn't prepare them for life. If an eighteen-year-old is pulled over by a cop for doing twenty miles per hour over the speed limit, it's unlikely the officer is going to yell at your kid or berate them for the incident. They're going to treat your child with respect. They'll write a ticket, and then they'll tell your child to have a nice day.

That's how the real world works. When you step across a line, there are consequences, not an attitude. That's why a consequence such as losing a privilege is a lot healthier than a parent losing their temper.

You use shame to discipline your toddler.

When handling a toddler's missteps, it's imperative you not make it personal. Shame is what your child feels when you give them the impression *they're* bad because they did something bad. It's damaging for your toddler, and it has many consequences later on in life.

Research has shown that shaming a toddler results in a massive fear of failure as an adult. That type of fear of failure creates issues at work and in their personal relationships. Beyond that, it teaches your child to think in black and white terms. A person's value seems tied to their actions, so they can be confused about their personal worth and the worth of others.

You pay bail for your toddler.

Some parents make the mistake of cleaning up after their toddler's mistake. Rather than helping your toddler face the consequence of their behavior, they shoulder the consequence instead. It doesn't seem like it's a big deal when your toddler is just two, but it is.

Paying for the candy bar your toddler shoplifted without making them apologize to the cashier is an example. Replacing the toy they broke in the middle of their temper tantrum is another.

However, here's the issue. Over time, your toddler will expect you to bail them out for what they did wrong. Eventually, you might end up paying real bail. While it might be imperative for you, as a parent, to decide how much of the natural consequences of the behavior your toddler can handle at this age, allowing them to experience absolutely no consequences teaches them they can behave however they want.

So you've seen a lot of examples of how you shouldn't discipline your toddler, but what are the proper ways to discipline a child so young? Let's look at that in the following chapter.

Chapter Five – Discipline Strategies for Toddlers

So what does it mean to discipline a toddler? Some people believe this equates to giving a spanking and punishments, but that's not what discipline is. Discipline is about setting rules to keep your toddler from engaging in aggressive behavior, dangerous behavior, and inappropriate behavior. It's about making sure you follow through with the consequences when he or she breaks those rules. In this chapter, you're going to learn seven strategies that will help you set the limits and stop a toddler's bad behavior without resorting to punishments and spankings.

#1 Pick Battles

If you're always telling your toddler 'no,' then your toddler is going to tune out this word and not understand your priorities. In addition, you can't follow through with all of those 'no's.' Define what a priority to you is, set your limits, and follow through with the same consequences. Ease up on the little things that are kind of annoying, but fall into that 'who cares' category. For example, does your toddler like to wear a certain color all the time, or maybe they like to play a certain game all the time? Ease up on that and allow them to do it.

#2 Know Their Triggers

Some misbehavior from toddlers is completely preventable, as long as you anticipate what's going to spark their behavior. If you do, then you can make a game plan in advance, such as removing the temptations from them. This strategy works well if your toddler is fixated on misbehaving the same way every time. For example, if you know your toddler is going rip the candy off the shelves at the checkout line in the store, then put them in the cart where they can't reach the candy to make sure they can't get into trouble. Sometimes, avoidance is the better option.

If your toddler tends to grab cans off the grocery store shelves, then bring some toys along for them to play with in the cart as you shop. If your toddler doesn't share during playdates, then remove the specific toys he or she doesn't want to share from the play area. If your toddler likes to draw on the walls, then stash the crayons out of their reach when you're not supervising them during drawing time.

#3 Be Consistent

During the toddler stage, children are working hard to comprehend how their behavior impacts those around them. If your reaction to a situation changes all the time, you'll confuse your toddler with mixed signals. For example, if you allow your toddler to throw a ball in the house one day and change your mind the next, it's pretty confusing for their developing minds.

There isn't a timetable as to how many misbehaviors and consequences it will take before a toddler stops a certain behavior. However, if you respond the same way all the time, then they will learn the lesson after a few times. Consistency is the key for most toddlers.

A special warning for parents who have the cutesy toddler. All toddlers are cute, but if your toddler likes to use their cuteness to distract you, don't let them! This teaches them they can use this type of behavior to get away with anything, even as adults.

#4 Don't Become Emotional

It's difficult to stay calm when your toddler refuses to brush their teeth for the hundredth time in a row that week, or when they pull on the dog's tail after you told them not to six times that day. However, if you scream in anger, the message you send is lost in the escalating situation. When your toddler is flooded with your negative emotions, your toddler sees the emotions and doesn't understand what you're saying. They're too focused on the entertainment value of seeing you scream and yell as if you were the one throwing a fit, which you are. Therefore, resist that urge to raise your voice, count to three as you take a deep breath, and get down to their eye level. The reprimand for their behavior should be done in an even, but serious, tone.

#5 Keep It Short and Simple

For most first-time parents, they tend to reason with their toddler when they break the rules, offering a detailed explanation of what happened and issuing detailed threats about the privileges that will be lost if the toddler doesn't stop their bad behavior. However, as a discipline strategy, over-talking is just as bad as becoming overly emotional.

While your toddler lacks the cognitive ability to understand your very complex sentences, your two- to three-year-old still lacks the attention span even if they have the language skills. Instead of speaking in long, complex sentences, communicate in short phrases, restating them a couple of times, and incorporating inflections in your tone and your facial expressions.

For example, if your toddler gives you a good swat to the knee, say, "No, Julie! Don't hit Mommy/Daddy! That hurts. No hitting. No hitting." As they get older, say around three, you can start incorporating the consequences into the sentence, but keep it simple the younger they are.

#6 Give Time-Outs

Time-outs should be used when repeated redirections, reprimands, and loss of privileges don't cure your toddler's negative behavior. Time-outs are one of the best discipline methods for children this age, but before you impose the time-out, make sure to put on your serious face and give a warning in a stern voice. If your toddler doesn't listen during the countdown of three to one, then it's time to go to the time-out room or chair.

Remember, make sure not to talk to your toddler during this time. This is their time to reflect on what they did wrong. When the time-out is over, you can ask them to apologize to you, and when they do, give them a big hug to let them know you're no longer angry with them. Toddlers don't like to be separated from their parents and toys, so time-outs tend to work really well at this age. Enjoy them while they work!

#7 Stay Positive

No matter how frustrating your toddler's behavior is, don't vent about their bad behavior in front of them. If you heard your boss say something really negative about you at work, then you'd lose respect for your boss. It's the same thing when your toddler hears you talking about them in a negative or hopeless way. If they don't have a good image of you as the boss, then they end up repeating their negative behavior.

Still, it's normal to feel exasperated. In fact, if you don't feel exasperated from time to time, then your toddler is an alien. On a more serious note, you should turn to a friend, pediatrician, or a spouse for support and advice when you feel overwhelmed.

In this next section, we'll look at the appropriate tactics for the different age stages of toddlers.

Appropriate Discipline for Different Ages

Disciplining your child effectively will all depend on what age range your toddler falls into. Let's take a look at the guides for eighteen months, two years, and three years to figure out how you should be disciplining your child.

Eighteen Months

At this age, your child is fearless, mobile, curious, impulsive, and clueless about all the consequences of their actions, which is definitely a recipe for trouble. They're exercising independence while still needing reassurance at the same time, which is a tricky equilibrium to maintain. It's a lot like this. Your eighteen-month-old baby is running down the hall away from you, but he or she is still looking over their shoulder to make sure you're there if they need you.

While your toddler is building vocabulary at this stage and is able to follow the simplest of instructions, they cannot effectively communicate what they want and cannot understand your lengthy reprimands. Your toddler might bite or hit to get your attention or to let you know they're upset. Consequences of misbehaving at this age have to be immediate. Waiting just five minutes to react to what happened will confuse your toddler because they won't understand why you're reprimanding them. They won't tie the consequence to the action.

Two Years

At this age, your toddler is using their growing motor skills to test the limits by jumping, running, throwing, and climbing things. They're speaking a few words right now, and become frustrated when they can't get their point across to you. This is the age where they're prone to tantrums. Your toddler is self-centered at this stage and doesn't like to share.

People tend to call this stage the terrible twos, but it's really more like the autonomous twos. Consequences during this age must be swift because your toddler does not have a sense of time yet. Since they still lack impulse control, give them another chance soon after the incident has occurred.

Three Years

Your toddler has now become very talkative and uses language to argue their point of view. They love to be around other children, and a have a lot of energy, so they have a hard time playing quietly at home at this age. Taking your three-year-old to karate classes, dance classes, or to the gym gives them the social interaction they're craving, and allows them to release that excess energy.

At this age, your toddler needs interaction with other children as much as they need affection from you and food. It is not a want, but a necessity. Your toddler knows right from wrong at this stage, understands actions and consequences, and retains information for many hours. Consequences can be delayed to get the maximum impact, and explanations can contain more detail. For example, if your toddler throws cereal at you, remind your toddler about the no-food-throwing rule, and then explain that if he does this again, he won't get to watch his favorite show. When he asks to watch television, let him or her know that they cannot because they threw food earlier today.

Conclusion

The most important thing you can do as a parent is to exercise patience and emotional control during your toddler's not-so-cute moments. Remember, you are raising a child that will soon grow into an adult, and this stage is one of the most important ones in their life when it comes to mental, emotional, and physical development. Sure, you can make a mistake here and there, maybe even lose your cool for a few moments in another room, but make sure the bulk of your child's discipline is with a calm, patient, and firm tone.

There will be times you'll want to throw in the proverbial towel (or the real one if bath time isn't so fun), but the good times are surely going to outweigh the teachable moments where you have to feel like the mean parent. And during those times when you feel like you have to be Bad Mommy or Bad Daddy, remember that the skills you're teaching your toddler now are going to help them for the rest of their lives. It's worth a little emotional discomfort now in order to see your baby grow into a wonderful man or woman later on.

They may not remember the specifics, but they'll remember how you were there for them to teach them the basics of life, and knowing you were there for them is the beauty of parenthood.

I hope you enjoyed the information you found in this book. If you did, please leave a review at your online eBook retailer's website.

Thank you for reading, and happy parenting!

Your Free Gift

I wanted to show my appreciation that you support my work so I've put together a free gift for you.

<u>Bonus – Daily Routine for Toddlers</u>

Just visit the link above to download it now.

I know you will love this gift.

Thanks!

Merry Palmer

Made in the USA
San Bernardino, CA
04 May 2020